TEN COMMANDMENTS

TEN SESSION OUTLINES
FOR CHILDREN

NICK HARDING

Kevin
Mayhew

First published in 2000 by
KEVIN MAYHEW LTD
Buxhall
Stowmarket
Suffolk IP14 3BW

0 1 2 3 4 5 6 7 8 9

ISBN 1 84003 645 1
Catalogue No. 1500392

Cover design by Jonathan Stroulger
Illustrations by Simon Smith
Edited by Katherine Laidler
Typesetting by Louise Selfe
Printed in Great Britain

Contents

About the author

Nick Harding grew up in Birmingham, found faith at a Baptist Church, spent student days in Devon, taught for a few years near Nottingham, and has been up to his eyes in children's and youth work ever since! He lives near Sherwood Forest with his wife and two energetic sons, loves the music of Elton John and Elgar, supports Aston Villa, is a member of the Mothers' Union, and travels on buses as a hobby! He works for his local cathedral, Southwell Minster, as Schools Officer where he also runs an award-winning educational project called 'Time Travelling!' He loves preaching, which he does every Sunday at churches of most denominations and traditions. Best recent moment – being really busy with a new challenge. Worst recent moment – fluffing the first line of a 'thought for the day' on BBC local radio!

Introduction _____

- Have you ever been stuck for material, and found that the time you put aside to plan has vanished?
- Have you ever struggled to use published material because it assumes the children have good Bible knowledge?

These are problems faced by everyone who works with children, whether in church or school. These session outlines are designed to meet your needs, with easy-to-prepare and varied material, including plenty of activity and lots for children to think about. They are aimed at children on the fringe of the church and those outside – perhaps who come to a holiday club, attend a midweek group, or go to the Christian group at school. They are intended for the 7-12 age group, but are adaptable for use with both younger and older groups. All the material here has been tried and tested over a number of years, and should provide all you need to help young people with no church experience get to grips with the nature of the Christian faith and ultimately God's love for them.

Each outline follows the same pattern, giving a number of sections which can be used. Remember that there is probably too much for one session, and you may want to miss items out or do them the following time. Other suggestions may be unsuitable for your group or facilities.

Theme   At the start of each outline is a clearly defined theme. This is to help you understand the point that the games, stories and talk suggestions are working towards.

Active game   There is at least one active game suggestion during each outline. This is provided to enable the young people to let off steam in a fun way, with a connection to the theme of the session.

Game   There is often another game which involves some of the group. Be aware that when asking for 'volunteers' you need to aim for a balance of boys and girls, able and less able, and so on.

Illustration   There are simple illustrations for a leader to act out included in some of these outlines. They introduce the theme of the session.

Quiz Many of the outlines have a quiz suggestion to enable you to reinforce the point, or to introduce the theme. These are not meant to be too competitive, and shouldn't be taken too seriously!

Discussion A vital skill to learn is the ability to express a point of view in a supportive environment. Discussion suggestions are provided to help you explore the theme and develop the children's skills in giving and receiving information.

Talk Rather than having a discussion it is sometimes necessary for you to be clear about what you want to say. Some outlines include talks, with the main points listed.

Craft These outlines include a craft suggestion where suitable and relevant. Most children learn best by doing, so it's good to include as much activity as possible in your plans. The craft suggestions include a minimum of equipment and resources.

Bible input Every outline includes a Bible reference and a suggestion as to how you may want to tell the story. Remember that the children may be unfamiliar with the Bible, and it should always be presented in a positive and lively manner.

Prayer At the end of each outline is a prayer or a prayer suggestion. These vary from being a quiet time for thought and meditation to being lively, aimed at children who are not used to praying and who may be embarrassed by it.

Memory chant Each outline includes a simple chant on the theme of that day. These could be learned, remembered, repeated each session and added to as you go along, giving all the group members some basic truths to remember. They are cumulative, so that by the end of the ten sessions the children will be able to say all the ten commandments in modern language.

Songs There are suggested songs given, but don't be restricted by this list. Most of them can be found in a large number of books from various publishers including
ICC *Spring Harvest Big Book of Kids' Praise*
Scripture Union *Everybody Praise*

HarperCollins *Junior Praise*

Kevin Mayhew *Kidsource*

You may know and use much more relevant and suitable songs!

Funsheet

This is for you to photocopy and use either as part of the session or to give the children to take home and complete. It complements the session but does not have to be used at the same time. Ingredients include wordsearches, questions, puzzles, prayers, thought starters and quizzes.

You need to add . . .

(a) time for registration, notices, chatting, tuck shop, and whatever else is a normal part of your regular meetings.

(b) your own wisdom, energy and creativity to make these outlines work for you and your young people.

Other suggestions

• Use these outlines for a holiday club, decorating the room with '10 Com' and using it on the publicity posters and leaflets.

• Use the chant '10 Com – God's Guidelines' to a regular clapping rhythm. This helps reinforce the teaching message for the ten outlines.

• If you have limited time each week split each of the sessions into two, providing a balance of activity and quiet in each.

• Try saying 'Amen' in a different way – shouting, winding up (ameeeeeeeeen), 'I agree' or 'Hey, that's cool!'

I hope *Ten Commandments* helps you do your job with children more effectively, and I pray that through it more young people will come to know the guidance and love that God offers for themselves.

With special thanks to
Clare, Callum and Jared

For all children's workers who
want to reach children for Jesus

Session 1	# Com 1 – One God

Theme

'I am the Lord your God.'

God tells us that there is only one true God.

Active game

Random rules

Make sure all the children are in the middle of the room. They must then obey everything you tell them all to do, however silly or strange that seems to be:

- stand on one leg and shout
- run around the room silently
- shake the hands of seven other people
- lie on the floor and whistle
- kneel down and clap your hands
- run around the room and touch all the walls
- sit down, stand up, and repeat
- pull an ugly face and crawl across the floor

Talk

The rules you just had to act out are silly rules and didn't make much sense. But most of the rules we have in life are for our own good. We may have rules at home, like doing certain jobs or coming home at the right time. At school there are rules such as not running in the corridors and being quiet when you are asked to. God gives us rules to live by, and they are good rules. They are guidelines to make sure that we live our lives as God designed them. God's rules, the Ten Commandments, are the best rules for us to follow.

Discussion

What if . . .

Read out some or all of these rules, each time allowing the children time to discuss what would happen if the rule was ignored:

- don't run in the school corridor
- look before you cross the road
- keep the music quiet in your bedroom
- don't take things that don't belong to you
- use lights on your bike at night
- keep out of the building site

Discussion and activity

You will need:

- pens and pencils
- small sheets of paper
- a large sheet of paper, scroll-like

Talk about the importance of rules in the group. Ask what would happen if everyone came along and did just what they wanted.

Split the group into threes and give each young person a sheet of paper and a pen. Ask them all to write down three or four rules which they think would be good for the group. Then ask the smaller groups to discuss them together and come up with the rules they think are the most important. These should be written up on the large sheet of paper and then put on the wall to remind the group of the rules they came up with.

Story

The only God

During the telling of this story (1 Kings 18:1-40) ask the children to put thumbs up each time you mention *Elijah* and down each time you mention *Baal*.

The people in the country where *Elijah* lived didn't take much notice of God. They ignored all the rules which God had told people it is best to follow, and they worshipped a pretend god called *Baal*. So God decided to speak to one of his messengers, a man called *Elijah*, and ask him to tell the people to listen to God and do what he said, but they ignored him. They listened to the prophets of *Baal* instead.

God told *Elijah* to go to the top of a mountain with the prophets of *Baal* and the people. There *Elijah* built an altar and a special bonfire to worship God, and the followers of the pretend god, *Baal*, built themselves an altar too. Then *Elijah* said, 'If God is the one real God, then you should worship him. The God who sends fire on to these bonfires is the real one.'

All day the prophets of *Baal* prayed, danced, and sang songs to worship *Baal*, but nothing happened. They tried even harder, crying out and ripping their clothes, but still nothing happened. Then *Elijah* called all the people to him. He poured water all over his bonfire, making it even harder to light, and then he prayed. 'Dear Lord God, send fire,' he prayed, 'so that all the people will know that your rules are good and you are the one true God'. A soon as *Elijah* had finished, the whole bonfire and the ground around it instantly became fire, and the people were amazed. They said, 'Now we know that *Baal* is not a real God, and that *Elijah's* God is the one true God'. After that most of the people followed God's rules because they knew he was the only God, the number one!

Talk

God proved that he was real, and that he was the only one. Christians believe that there is only one true God, and he loves everyone. He wants us all to have a really good life by following his rules.

Memory chant

This is the first of the 10 that go together to make a modern version of the 10 commandments:

He is the only God.

Prayer idea

You will need:

- a candle
- matches

Ask the children to keep their eyes open and look at the candle. Remind them that the one real God sent flames to prove that he is real, and ask them to think about how much they love the one true God.

Songs

Great is the one
O Lord, you're great
God is here, God is here
God is good, God is great

1. One God.

Remember—there is only one real God.

reif

yardpe

prihswedop

prihswedop

yardep

nephdeap

Elijah _____ God, but the other people _____ Baal.

Elijah _____ to God, and the other people _____ to Baal.

God sent _____ and flames, but nothing _____ to the other altar.

Chant
He is the only God...

FATHERGOD

Write out who the ONE GOD is...

_ _ _ _ _ _
_ _ _ _ .

Session 2   Com 2 – Real worship _____

Theme   'Worship no God but me.'

God is the only one worth worshipping, and we shouldn't worship anything as much as him.

Active game   *Where to buy?*

You will need:

- labels on four walls: Supermarket, Bank, Garage, Clothes shop

As you read out the following story stop at each * to allow the group time to run to the correct wall and stand still there. You could make it a little more competitive by excluding the child or children who get there last or go to the wrong wall.

There was a man who really loved having money * and spent his money on really good things like new cars * and really smart, expensive clothes *. He also spent loads of money on food *, and he would buy nothing but the best food *. He wore his clothes * as he drove around in his latest car *, and thought he was the best person in the world. In fact, he worshipped his car *. He spent most of his spare time polishing it, looking at it and taking photos of it. It was the cleanest car * in town. Every Sunday he spent hours cleaning his car *, and thought there was nothing better than it. But he also liked food *, and spent much of his time producing very fancy meals * and looking at the great food *. Then there were the clothes *, which cost a lot of money; money which he got from the bank *. He really looked after his clothes, spending a lot of time making sure they were hung up properly, and deciding what clothes * to wear.

With all his money *, and the food *, clothes *, and cars *, this man had lots of things which he worshipped. He thought all of those four things, money *, food *, clothes *, and cars * were the most important things there could be.

Talk   There are many things which are really important to us, and we want to spend time and money on them. But if they take over all of our lives they become the things that we worship, and they become more important than anything else.

Discussion   Ask the children to tell you and the others in the group what they really think about the following things, looking at each

13

one in turn. If possible have a real one there, or at least a picture of each:

video games	computer games
football	bike
fashionable clothes	cars
boy bands	girl bands
TV	Pokémon or other popular collectable cards

Story

Wrong worship

Tell the story of the people of Israel making a golden calf (Exodus 32) in your own words or using a story Bible. Make sure you cover the following points:

- Moses was the leader of the people, and he had left them safely at the base of a mountain while he went up the mountain to speak with God.

- The people became scared because they didn't know when Moses was coming back to lead them.

- They nagged and moaned to Aaron, Moses' brother, until he agreed to make a new god for them to worship.

- Aaron told the people to hand in their gold jewellery and he melted it down to put into a mould and produce a golden calf.

- The people thought the golden calf was the most important thing in their lives, and they worshipped it. They spent time looking at it, they cleaned and polished it, and they loved it.

- God told Moses to go back down to the people and stop them worshipping something else.

- Moses and God were angry with the people because they had decided to worship a golden calf instead of worshipping God.

Craft

You will need:

- thin card, bright yellow or orange if possible

- white paper

- thick red marker pens

Firstly the children should take a sheet of orange or yellow paper and draw on it the shape of a calf. This should then be cut out and stuck on to the centre of a sheet of white paper. Using the marker pens they should then draw a large circle around it, and put a diagonal line across it in the manner of a road sign. To add to the image the group members could write 'Don't worship' underneath the sign.

Quiz   You will need nine small golden calf shapes similar to those made in the craft activity. Split the group into two, and ask each half a question in turn, awarding a golden calf for each correct answer:

1. Who was the leader of the people?   Moses
2. Where had the leader gone?   up the mountain
3. What happened to the people?   got scared
4. Who was Aaron?   Moses' brother
5. What did the people give Aaron?   gold jewellery
6. What did he do with it?   melted it
7. What animal shape did they worship?   calf
8. Who told Moses what the people were doing?   God
9. How did Moses react to the people?   angry

Game   *Two voices*

Ask for two volunteers to come to the front. They must have a conversation with each other about the subject without stopping or hesitating, for one minute. If they manage it they should get a sweet or other small prize. Repeat the activity with another pair, and so on as time allows.

Subjects: computer games, TV, pocket money, cars.

Talk   We might really enjoy things like money, food or a particular pop group. There is nothing wrong with enjoying things, as long as they don't take us over and become the most important thing in our lives. Some people worship their car, always cleaning it and looking after it. Other people worship money, and always want to have more of it. We might worship pro-grammes on TV and computers, and spend more time on them than other things.

God calls us all to worship him. His people ignored him and made a calf out of gold, while we ignore him by making other things more important. God is the only God and the best thing we can do is worship him.

Memory chant   Add this one to the last:

Don't worship the odd.

15

Prayer Say this prayer, stopping and being silent at * to allow the young people to think about the things that are important to them:

Thank you, Father God, that you love us.
Thank you for all the things that we really enjoy, like * .
Help us to enjoy them but not worship them.
Help us to always worship you.
Amen.

Songs We worship you
I love you, Lord Jesus
Father, we adore you
Lord, we've come to worship you

2. Real Worship.

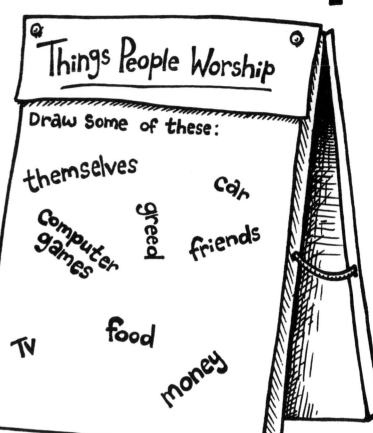

Things People Worship

Draw some of these:

themselves   car

        greed
Computer   friends
games

TV   food

                money

Chant

Don't worship the odd.

THE CALF. Number the Pictures...

THE PEOPLE SAID

We now worship this model of a calf

THE PEOPLE SAID

We don't know when Moses will come back

AARON SAID

Let's melt our jewellery and make a calf.

God wants us to worship only him.

Session 3   Com 3 – Best name _____

Theme
'Do not misuse my name.'

God's name is special, and we shouldn't say it or use it wrongly.

Active game
Each person should be wearing badges with their first and last names on (sticky labels will do). Ask all the children to stand in the middle of the room and then move around to find:

- someone with the same name
- someone with both of the same initials
- someone with one of the same initials
- someone with the same name as your brother/sister
- someone with the same name as one of your parents

Introduction
Names are very important, and most of us want people to use our name properly. We don't want people to make fun of our names or pronounce them wrongly. We usually like our names, but even if we don't they still say something about us and make us different from the people around us.

In the times of the Bible, names were often much more important. All names had meanings, and they could describe good or bad. One of Jesus' friends was called Simon but Jesus renamed him Peter, which means 'rock'. Jesus said that on the rock of Peter, the good foundation, he would build his Church.

Activity   *My name*

You will need as many baby names books as possible. You'll probably be able to borrow them from couples who are expecting or who have a young baby.

Ask the group to get into pairs or threes and look up the names of the others in the group. Many of the names will have meanings, so the others should decide if the names really represent the person.

Story 1   *Moses and 'I am'*

Tell the story of Moses and the burning bush (Exodus 3:1-14) in your own words. Make sure you cover the following points:

- Moses had run away and settled in a new country.
- He didn't want to be a leader.

- He was looking after the sheep when the bush started to burn, and Moses went to it.

- He noticed that the bush was not burning up and becoming ashes.

- The bush spoke to him, and told him to go and lead the people.

- Moses made many excuses, but God's voice answered all his questions.

- Moses asked who the voice was, and God said, 'I am who I am . . . the God called "I am" has sent you.'

Game *Names*

Ask for two volunteers to come to the front. In turn ask them to complete the following names with the surnames or first names. The name they must guess is in brackets, and if they struggle you can give clues:

(Chris) Tarrant	(Pete) Sampras
Queen (Elizabeth II)	Victoria and David (Beckham)
Sir Cliff (Richard)	(Blue) Peter
Tony (Blair)	(William) Hague
(Jon) Bon Jovi	Mel (C)
Walt (Disney)	Robbie (Williams)

Talk Names help us identify ourselves. God told Moses to use the name 'I am' to describe God, because there is only one God, and he is the real one. When we use God's name wrongly, like when we swear or mutter 'God' under our breath, we are hurting God, and he feels as bad as we do when people make fun of our names.

Story 2 This story, from Acts 3:1-10, can be told from a story Bible or as a short drama sketch between two people. The full script for the drama is below:

Two men limp to the front, and sit looking at each other.

1 Hello there, how are you doing?

2 Oh, fine thanks. You know, I've been begging on these Jerusalem streets for years now, and still people walk straight past me and don't help.

1 Ah, well, it all depends where you beg. Up at the Beautiful Gate near the temple you can get some good money, especially from those who want to show off to their religious friends.

2 Well, you must have heard what happened up there this afternoon, three-ish, I think.

1 No, I've heard nothing. Tell me more.

2 Well, apparently there were two of those chaps from Galilee, followers of that Jesus who they say came alive from the dead. They were on their way to the temple when old Jack, you know him . . .

1 Oh yes, Jack. He always waits there. He's never been able to walk, has he?

2 No, you're right. He was born lame. Jack called out to the two Jesus followers and they stopped and spoke to him. They said they hadn't any money, but they would give him something better.

1 What can be better for a beggar than money?

2 Hang on! They told him to get up and walk in the name of Jesus. They said his name had power, and Jack did.

1 Did what?

2 Got right up, there and then, and walked, jumped and skipped. It was something to see, I can tell you!

1 And it was all because of the name of Jesus?

2 Yes, the name's got power!

1 Well, I think I'll have to find out more about this. Sounds good to me!

Talk God's name should not be used wrongly and wasted, because it has power. We should be careful what we say so that we don't upset God by using his name wrongly. Even today people are healed when others pray for them, as long as they use the name of God or Jesus. We don't have the power to heal people ourselves, but the name of God has real power. We should always use the name properly and not waste it, because it is very special.

Memory chant This is the third in the series:

Be careful what you say.

Prayer Pray with the following response: *help me love your name.*

Dear God,
When I am angry and I want to swear
help me love your name.

When I want to shout out something
help me love your name.
When I need some help and power from you
help me love your name.
When I need someone to turn to
help me love your name.
Amen.

Songs   Your name is Jesus
God has got a plan
He is the Lord
My God is so big

3. Best Name.

Don't waste God's Special name!

My Factfile

My name is _____
_____

I think my name means _____
_____

_____

_____

_____

_____

my Photo

Chant

Be careful what you say...

the LAME MAN said...

'Please _____
_____
_____
_____
_____
_____ .'

GOD SAID...

_ _ _ _ _ _ _
(write it down!)

PETER replied...

'In the name of _____
_____
_____
_____
_____
_____ .'

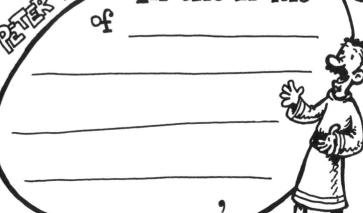

Session 4   Com 4 – Special day _____

Theme   'Remember my special day and keep it holy.'

God expects us to put time aside to worship him. Sundays are often days when people worship God, and we should follow that example.

Active game   *Time*

Ask the children to stand and then act out what they do at different times of the day. Some of them could concentrate on a week day, and others on a weekend. Try to identify some of the things being acted out, and point out any that are particularly interesting or funny.

Craft activity   You will need:

- split pins
- card
- pens, felt tips or crayons
- scissors, compasses

Give each child a large sheet of card and ask them, with the help of a compass, to draw a circle on it. Then ask them to write the numbers on the clock face and do small drawings next to their busy times to illustrate what they do at those times. They should then cut out the clock face and use the scraps of card to make two clock hands. These can be fixed on using the split pin.

Introduction   Hold up a clock. Explain that for most people there is not enough time, and we end up rushing around and being too busy. When we are busy there are some things that get forgotten. We may not be as tidy as we should be, or we may not have time to wash properly. Most of all, many people forget to make time for God.

Activity   *Stop*

You will need a whistle. Ask the group to walk around and then stop each time they hear the whistle and stand still. They should be really quiet and think about the word you say (see below). Then clap your hands to let them walk around again, before blowing the whistle again and repeating the exercise.

Words you should say:

quiet	peace
work	busyness
time	tiredness

Talk

God designed us, so he knows what is good for us. In the Bible story of when God made the world he rested after he had finished it, and told us that we should rest for a day too. It would be horrible to have to go to school every day including weekends, wouldn't it? We all need to take time off, even if we are young. Then we have the energy to work hard and do our best for ourselves and others the rest of the time.

In the Bible the day that people put aside to rest and worship God is called the Sabbath, but most people now know it as Sunday. That is why most churches meet on Sundays, and why Sunday is the day when many people do not have to go to work. Jesus followed most of the rules about the special day, but some people thought he had done wrong on one Sabbath.

Discussion

You will need paper and pens. In smaller groups ask the young people to talk about and list all the things they could do on a Sunday. Some of the group will be from families which do not see Sunday as being different, so you need to remember to be sensitive with this. Once they have all made lists bring the group back together again and go through them. Ask them to think whether they feel tired or refreshed after doing lots of things at weekends, and whether all the activity leaves any time to be quiet and think about God.

Story

Jesus on the Sabbath

This is found in Luke 13:10-17. Explain that the religious officials always wanted to catch Jesus out, and they thought he had broken the old rule that said people shouldn't work on the Sabbath. But Jesus was helping someone who had suffered from evil making her ill for a long time, and Jesus thought helping her was a really good thing to do.

Read the story from an appropriate translation that the children will understand, such as the Good News, CEV or Children's Bible. You may want to use children to play some of the parts (the lame woman, officials, Jesus) and move them around as you tell the story. Tell the group that they need to listen especially carefully if you plan to do the quiz.

Quiz

Say that again

Sit the group on the floor. Read out the same story (Luke 13:10-17), missing out the last word of each sentence. The first child to stand and shout out the correct word should be given a small prize (a sweet for instance) before moving on to the next sentence.

Talk

Cover the following points:

- God knows we all need to rest, and for most of us that day of rest should be Sunday.
- God told all people to keep one day special and different so that we can think about him.
- Jesus believed that it was right to do good anytime, and set us an example of loving others all the time.
- We should think carefully about the time we give to God.

Prayer activity

You will need pens and paper. Ask each of the group to write on a piece of paper one thing they do each day or most days. Then pray this prayer, going around the group so that each group member in turn fills in the gap and all the others say the first part of the line in italics:

God, you know what we do,
and you know what is best for us.
God, I know you are with me when . . .
Thank you that you are with me all the time.
Help me to make time for you.
Amen.

Memory chant

This is the fourth of the set:

Have a restful day.

Songs

I will enter his gates
I will dance, I will sing
Sing praise
And God said

10 Com

4. Special Day.

God wants us to keep a day special.

JESUS ON THE SABBATH

Link the words with the pictures.

One Sabbath, Jesus was telling people about God.

A woman wanted to be healed from her bad back.

Jesus healed her.

Some leaders were angry with Jesus.

Jesus told them that it was right to do good on God's Special day.

SUNDAY

(circle) what you do on a Sunday.

Underline what God wants us to do.

do good
worship
shop
care
go to church
play
rest
work
talk
visit
parks

Chant

Have a restful day.

Session 5 Com 5 – Honour parents _____

Theme

'Honour your father and mother.'

God wants us to show respect to those close to us, including our parents.

Note

The themes of 'parents' and 'family' need to be handled carefully during this session. Please be aware of those in the group who may be in painful home situations.

Active game

Get into . . .

Ask the group to stand and then get into groups of the number you say, pretending to be the animal you say. Here are some suggestions, but it is easy to make up your own.

group of 3 – monkeys   group of 2 – people
group of 5 – elephants   group of 7 – kangaroos
group of 4 – sheep   single – lion

Introduction

Have some old family photographs to show the group. Talk through who is who, and where you are at what age. Explain that, like the animal groups in the game, families come in all different shapes and sizes and none are right or wrong. God wants us all to be in a loving family and he knows how families work best for everyone, but sometimes it doesn't work out like that.

Craft

My family

You will need:

- A4 paper

- pens, felt tips or crayons

- small 'lick and stick' triangles

Give each child a sheet of paper and ask them to fold it into four and open it again. These are the four 'photos' of their family in different situations which they should now draw. The triangles of paper can be used at the corners of each drawing to make it look a little more like a real photo.

Talk

There are times when parents seem to be really good. We might think they are wonderful when they are kind to us or when we're having fun. But they are not so good when they tell us to do things we don't want to do, or when they get angry with us.

God clearly tells all people that it is best to honour parents by doing what they say and showing respect. This is hard, but they are not perfect and do make mistakes too. Most parents do their best, and don't deliberately make things hard for their children.

Game

What happens?

Ask for up to 8 volunteers to line up across the front. Each one must choose a number from 1 to 10 and then take the consequences. Some of the things will be nice, while others will be more unpleasant!

1. Get a round of applause.

2. Everyone cheers you.

3. You must hop around the room.

4. You do a bow while everyone shouts your name.

5. Do 20 star jumps.

6. Everyone boos and hisses.

7. You get a standing ovation.

8. You must tell a nursery rhyme.

Discussion

Start by commenting on the game, pointing out that the contestants didn't know what would happen after they had chosen a number. God knows what is best for us, and he tells us to honour our parents because he knows that if we don't, things could get bad for us. We do know the consequences of answering back or saying 'no' to our mum when she asks us to do a job.

Ask the group to split into twos or threes and talk about what happens to them if they do something to anger their parents. They should discuss the consequences and the ways to avoid getting into trouble.

Story

Joseph and his brothers

This is the account of Joseph and his bothers, taken from Genesis 37:1-11. You may want to show this from a video of the story or the video of the musical. These are the main points of the story you should cover:

- Joseph was one of 12 brothers, and there were probably sisters too.
- Jacob, his father, loved him and Joseph honoured his father.
- Joseph used the coat he was given to show off to his brothers.
- Joseph was a bit of a show-off and boasted about his dreams.
- His dreams showed his brothers bowing down to him.
- His brothers were angry and jealous.
- Jacob thought boasting was a bad thing to do.
- He thought about Joseph and his dreams.
- Joseph's brothers sold Joseph to be a slave.
- They dishonoured their father by telling him that Joseph had died.

Quiz   You will need paper and pens for all the children. This is a simple multiple choice quiz for all the children to try. As it is self-marked it does not need to be too competitive.

Everyone should have a piece of paper and pen, and should write either 1 or 2 for each answer. The answer in *italics* is the correct one.

Question 1.
How many brothers did Joseph have?
Answer 1   *11*   Answer 2   12

Question 2.
What was Joseph's father called?
Answer 1   Joachim   Answer 2   *Jacob*

Question 3.
What made his brothers jealous first?
Answer 1   dreams   Answer 2   *coat*

Question 4.
What did his brothers do in the dreams?
Answer 1   *bow down*   Answer 2   love Joseph

Question 5.
What did Joseph do that his father thought was bad?
Answer 1   *boasted*   Answer 2   smiled

Question 6.
What was Joseph sold to be?
Answer 1   a teacher   Answer 2   *a slave*

At the end go through the correct answers and ask the children to 'mark' their own. The results may not be entirely reliable, but it will be fun anyway!

Talk Joseph, his brothers and his father were like many families. God's ideal is that there are parents who love their children equally and that their children honour and respect their parents. Joseph didn't always honour his father, and instead boasted to him. His brothers didn't respect their father when they lied to him by telling him that Joseph was dead. Even their father Jacob got it wrong by showing more love for Joseph than his other sons. They became a very unhappy family, and they all ended up hurt and upset. God wants us to learn from their mistakes by doing all we can to honour our parents, however hard it may be.

Memory chant The latest chant to add to the others:

Honour Mum and Dad.

Prayer idea Ask the group to sit really quietly and think about their parents, both those they live with and others who may have moved away. From time to time say another of these sentences, designed to help them pray and think:

- Let's think of the good memories we have of our parents.
- We remember times when we have hurt or upset our mum or dad.
- We think about the times when they have made mistakes and upset us.
- Let's think of all the things they do for us and give us.
- We ask God to help us honour our mum and dad.

Songs Uh well, it's excellent to be obedient
Give thanks with a grateful heart
As for me and my house
God is good, God is great

Session 6   Com 6 – Love life _____

Theme 'Do not commit murder.'

God gives life, and it is special and precious. We should love life and do all we can to help others, not hurt them.

Active game *Mood walks*

Everyone should stand and walk around the room. When you shout out another mood, they should start to walk in that mood. There should be no noises and no sound affects! The moods you could choose are:

happy	rushed	lonely
sad	worried	in the rain
important	scared	relaxed
nervous	determined	hungry

Discussion Ask the group to think about their own brothers or sisters, or other close friends. Try to lead the discussion covering the following points:

- Brothers and sisters can be really good sometimes.

- Jealousy is usual between brothers and sisters.

- Siblings make us really angry sometimes, and we feel like hurting them!

- We should never use our anger to hurt other people.

- God expects us to love life and not hurt others, including brothers or sisters.

Story (Part 1) *Cain and Abel*

Read this version of the story – taken from Genesis 4:1-14 – or another from a suitable Bible translation. The group should do digging actions when farming and growing crops are mentioned, and stroking actions when the lambs are mentioned.

After Adam and Eve had settled in the Garden of Eden they let God down by doing wrong. Finally they settled in another land to grow food and there they started a family. Cain was the first one to be born, and Eve was very pleased indeed. She decided to give him the name Cain because it meant 'With God's help I have had a son'. Soon the little boy grew up, all the time showing interest in the farming and growing of crops which his father Adam did. Later there was another

35

baby, a brother for Cain. He was given the name Abel and grew up showing interest in the sheep and lambs which his father also kept. When they had both grown up Cain became a farmer, looking after his own land. Abel became a shepherd, looking after his own flocks of sheep.

Every year Adam and Eve, along with Cain and Abel, gave God an offering of the best crops and sheep to show how much they loved God and appreciated all he did for them. Cain brought some wheat, but it might not have been his best because God was angry with him. Abel brought his best lamb to God, and God was pleased. That's when the trouble really began.

Craft activity

Bad news collage

You will need:

- newspapers and magazines
- glue sticks and paper
- scissors

Ask the group to go through newspapers picking out bad news headlines and cutting them out. In particular they should look out for bad news stories which are about what people have done to each other. When they have lots of headlines they should stick them at random angles on a piece of paper to form a bad news collage.

Talk

Many people do bad things to others. They may hurt them or even kill them. Some of these stories are really horrible, but are not likely to happen to us. God gave the rule 'Don't murder' because he knows that there are people who want everything to go their way and get angry when it doesn't. Some people get jealous and hate others enough to kill them. We should love life and do all we can to be kind and helpful, not hurtful and cruel. We already know that Cain and Abel were brothers and that they gave offerings to God. Even people very close to us can get angry with us, and we can get angry with them. But in the story of these brothers things went very bad . . .

Story (Part 2)

Cain and Abel

As we already know, every year Adam and Eve, along with Cain and Abel, gave God an offering of the best crops and sheep to show how much they loved God and appreciated all he did for them. Cain brought some wheat, but it might not have been his best because God was angry with him. Abel brought his best lamb to God, and God was pleased.

36

Cain was very angry that God had not accepted his offering, but God said 'You are angry because you did what was wrong.' Later Cain was still really cross, and jealous that his younger brother Abel had succeeded in pleasing God, while he had failed. When they met near their home Cain said to his brother, 'Let's go for a walk in the fields.' And that's what they did. As they talked Cain got more and more jealous, until he took away the most precious thing Abel had – his life. Cain had murdered his brother, and God knew what he had done. God told Cain to move away and grow crops somewhere else. His punishment would be that he would never really settle anywhere.

Talk

We don't really know why Cain got so angry. He must have loved his brother, but he became so jealous of him that he killed him. God made life and he loves it. He doesn't want any of us to damage the life of others by hurting them or killing them. We must learn to live and pray for peace, and do our best to love life ourselves.

Prayer

Say this prayer, with the group listening quietly:

Dear God, help me to love all those close to me.
Help me to love my brothers and sisters.
Help me to do all I can to love life.

Dear God, help others to love those around them.
Help those who live in areas of war and hate.
Help and forgive those who have taken the life of someone.

Dear God, help all people to love life.
Help us to enjoy all that you give us.
Help us to enjoy being kind to others.
Amen.

Memory chant

The sixth chant of the series:

Don't murder or do bad.

Songs

I'm sorry
I'm special
We will turn our hearts
Love, love your enemies

6. Love Life.

God never wants us to hurt others.

Life is Good...

beca__se I have f__ends an__ __eople to l__k afte__ m__.
Life i__ __ood becau__e I k__w God re__ly lo__es me.

A	J	O	S	I	R	O	M	E	T
K	P	F	J	V	F	F	E	S	P
N	A	F	B	C	A	I	N	S	U
A	B	E	L	C	R	E	D	O	Z
L	P	R	I	O	M	L	A	N	D
R	K	I	L	L	E	D	F	S	Y
M	A	N	H	A	R	V	E	S	T
E	N	G	W	H	S	G	P	Q	X
P	N	B	B	R	O	T	H	E	R
E	V	I	L	A	S	T	M	O	P

Find these words from the story:
· CAIN · ABEL · FARMER · FIELD ·
· BROTHER · OFFERING · KILLED · LAND ·
· SONS · MEN · HARVEST · EVIL ·

FINISH THIS PRAYER

Thank you, God, that you made life. Help me to _____

_____

_____

_____

_____. Amen.

Chant

Don't murder or do bad.

Session 7   Com 7 – Be together _____

Theme

'Do not commit adultery.'

It is God's ideal that married people should stay together, and he wants people to really love each other.

Note

The themes of 'parents' and 'family' need to be handled carefully during this session. Please be aware of those in the group who may be in painful home situations.

Illustration

You will need:

- a pottery jug
- a glass jug
- blackcurrant juice

Put some blackcurrant juice into the pottery jug, but do not let the children see it. Then fill the glass jug with water, and explain that you are going to turn that water into blackcurrant juice. Pour the water into the pottery jug, and then back again into the glass jug.

Explain the way you made the water into blackcurrant, although many of the children will have worked it out already. Explain that Jesus really did turn water into something else.

Active game

Pairs games

Ask the children to get into pairs, preferably one boy and one girl in each pair. Then demonstrate and ask them to have a go at each of these exercises:

Trust walk	One of the pair keeps her eyes closed while the other leads her around the room. Then swap over.
Stand	Pairs sit on the floor back to back and link arms. Then they push against each other to stand up.
Wheelbarrow	One of the pair stands and holds the feet of the other, who then walks on their hands to form the shape of a wheelbarrow.

Discussion

Mention that in the games two people were needed for each. If the 'blind' person was on their own they would have got lost or hurt. If the wheelbarrow didn't have help it would not work. Then discuss other things that we all need help with.

Story   *The party at Cana*

Introduce the story by setting the scene. Wedding parties went on for many hours, and the best wine was used first, with the cheaper wine being kept till later. The very worst thing that could happen was to run out of food or wine. That would bring shame and embarrassment to the family. Jesus was invited to a wedding party, to see a man and a woman get married and make promises to be together for ever.

Read the story (John 2:1-11) from a suitable version of the Bible.

Talk   While you do this you may want to ask a couple (boy and girl) to come and stand at the front as if they are getting married.

Some of you will have been to weddings. You might even have been to the wedding of your mum to your new dad, or to the wedding of a brother or sister. Weddings are only the start of marriage, and God wants marriages to last for ever. When people get married they promise to try to stick together, because it is one of God's rules that adults who are married should stay together and not fall in love with someone else. But we all go wrong at times, and some adults find it really hard to keep those promises.

God loves everyone, and those adults who have not been able to stay together are still loved by God. He can help them through the pain and difficulties that breaking up bring.

Craft   *Invitation*

You will need:

- good quality paper or card

- pens and crayons

Ask the children to think back to the story of the wedding in Cana. They should then design the invitation that Jesus may have been sent asking him to go to the wedding. You could use this wording or similar (although the names and date are not correct):

Simeon and Ruth invite
Jesus of Nazareth
to their wedding.
The Feast House, Cana
Thursday, March 25th, AD 30
Please reply to the bride's parents

Memory chant

The chant on today's theme:

Adults – stay together.

Prayer idea

Ask the children to sit quietly and think about married couples they know. They could be their own parents, grandparents, neighbours or relatives. As they do so pray this prayer:

Father God, thank you that you know what is best for us.
You know it is best for couples to stay together.
Please help all the people we are thinking of now.
Amen.

Then ask the children to think about adults they know who have broken up from their partners. Again, they could be parents, relatives or friends. As they do so say this prayer:

Father God, thank you that you really care about us.
You know how people feel when things go wrong.
Please help all the people we are thinking of now.
Amen.

Songs

Let your love shine through
God is good, God is great
God has got a plan
Live my life by faith

Session 8 Com 8 – Honest hands

Theme
'Do not steal.'

We can all be tempted to take things that do not belong to us, but that is never a good thing to do.

Quiz
Guess what?

Ask the children to guess what you are describing as you read out the following clues. If they guess *hands* before you finish, continue anyway:

- They are an odd shape.
- They have soft bits, bones and lines.
- Most of us have two of them.
- The can cause pain and hurt.
- They can take things which don't belong to them.
- They can do good.
- They sometimes have a gold ring attached.
- They have a thumb each.
- We can wave them.

Introduction
Hands can be really good and really bad. In a few seconds I could use my hands to hurt somebody by hitting them, I could make someone feel good by patting them on the head, or I could clap using both hands. I could use my hands to give someone something really nice, or take something that doesn't belong to me. Hands can be destructive, and hands can do brilliant things.

Talk and activity
Using hands

Sit the group on the floor. Then read out this talk, asking the children to do what you are describing as you go along.

Hands do good, positive things. We can do some of them now. Let's try waving our hands at someone we haven't spoken to today. Now we could clap the person sitting next to us. A tap on the head or a gentle touch makes us feel loved and cared about. We could carefully offer a cup of tea or coffee to the person sitting in front of us. We can give something to the person sitting behind us. Hands can be really good, but they can cause pain too.

Story

You may want to have something that looks precious available, and use up to four children to help you tell this story. Encourage the children to learn and join in with you when you say, 'God told them not to touch anything'. It is based on Joshua 7.

The people of God had a great success. They had marched around the city of Jericho seven times as God had told them. Then the walls of the city had fallen down and the city was left for the people of God to take over. God spoke to all the people. God told them not to touch anything they found in the city. They should not take any money or jewels. They had to leave everything where it was.

A soldier came along to search all the houses and make sure that there were no people left there. As he looked he saw some precious jewels and said, 'I do like that.' But as he said it he remembered that God told them not to touch anything. So he left the treasure and walked away.

A second soldier came along, and after searching some houses he too saw the jewels. He looked at them carefully and then said, 'I do like that, I really do like that.' But then he remembered that God told them not to touch anything. So he left the treasure and walked away.

Then a third soldier came along and after searching some houses he too saw the jewels. He looked at them carefully and then said, 'I do like that, I really do like that, I really really do like that.' But then he remembered that God told them not to touch anything. So he left the treasure and walked away.

Finally a soldier called Achan came along. After he had searched some houses he too saw the jewels. He looked at them carefully and then said, 'I do like that, I really do like that, I really really do like that.' He remembered that God told them not to touch anything, but still he allowed his hands to touch and pick up the treasure. Once he had done that, he thought that it wouldn't matter if he took it, so he did.

The next day God talked to the people, telling them that someone had taken some of the treasure. The people were shocked – they knew that one of God's rules was that no one should take anything that didn't belong to them. Soon Achan realised that God knew what he had done, and he was punished for stealing.

Active game

Ask for five fit and athletic volunteers to come to the front. They are going to do a range of activities based on hands, and race to be the first to do them. The other children should watch and try to spot who is the first to do the action. Demonstrate them to the other children who will be watching.

- hands on heads
- shake 10 hands

- hands on toes
- handstands
- hands on the door
- hands in the air
- slap 10 hands
- hands giving

Discussion

Lead the group in talking about how easy it is to be tempted. Try to cover the following:

- We are all tempted – what tempts the children?
- God made the rule so that no one cheats others by taking things that are not theirs.
- We should try to remember what it feels like when our things are taken.
- We can't blame our hands – our brains tell them what to do!

Talk

We can all use our hands for good or bad. We might think it's fun to take something that belongs to someone else, until someone takes our belongings. We would all be better off keeping our hands to ourselves and not trying to take others' things.

Memory chant

Here is today's chant:

Don't steal things ever.

Prayer

Say this prayer twice, asking the group to listen carefully:

God,
help us never to cause pain and hurt.
Help us never to take anything that belongs to others.
Help us always to do good.
Amen.

Songs

Don't be an actor
I just want to thank you, Lord
God's people
Everything comes from God

8. Honest Hands.

Remember – taking other people's things is never right.

ACHAN

NUMBER THE THINGS THAT HAPPENED IN THE RIGHT ORDER.

I Want

CIRCLE THE THINGS YOU WOULD REALLY LIKE

○ Achan took the nice things.

God said, ① 'Don't take anything.'

Achan ○ owned up to his mistake.

○ Achan saw the nice things.

○ God told Joshua, who tried to find out who had taken things.

Chant

Don't steal things ever.

Session 9   Com 9 – Speak truth _____

Theme

'Do not say wrong things.'

God expects us to tell the truth and not lie to others.

Introduction

You will need a newspaper.

Hold up the newspaper and ask the children whether they think everything in it is true. Do they believe all the stories are true? There are many different newspapers every day, and although most of them have the same news in them they are not all being completely honest. Some want you to believe one thing, while others try to make you believe something else.

Active quiz

True or false?

Label a wall with the word 'true' and another with 'false'. The children should listen to the statement and decide if it is true or false, and move to the relevant wall. You could add your own true or false statements to these:

Elephants cannot jump.	true
The longest nose ever is 15cm.	false (18cm)
Jesus was born in a hospital.	false (stable)
The Bible has 66 books in it.	true
The human body has 206 bones.	true
The word 'and' is in the Bible 46,227 times.	true

Discussion

Ask the children to get into pairs or threes and discuss the following questions. It may help to copy these or write them up on a large sheet for them all to see:

• Do you believe everything other people tell you?

• Do you think it is right to tell lies?

• What lie have you told that you remember?

• How do you feel when you tell lies?

• What do you think God thinks when we tell lies?

Talk

One of God's ten rules for all people is that we should never tell lies. There are many reasons why God wants us to tell the truth. He knows that people get hurt and upset when they find out that someone has not been honest. He knows that it is wrong to pretend and say things that are not meant.

There are also many reasons why we may be tempted to lie. We may tell a lie to cover up something we have not done, or hide something that we have done which we know was wrong. We might tell a lie to trick someone, or scare them. We might even tell a lie because we are scared or worried, like the people in today's Bible story.

Story   *The spies*

This story comes from Numbers 13, and tells the story of honest and dishonest spies. You should read it from a story Bible or tell it in your own words. Ask the children to make their hands into binocular shapes around their eyes and look around every time you say 'spy' or 'spies'. Here are the main points to cover in this story:

- Moses was the leader of the people, and they were looking for more land.

- The next land was called Canaan, and God told them to look at it.

- God told Moses to send 12 spies ahead to look at the land.

- They had to find out about the strength of the army, the towns and cities, and whether the land was good to grow crops.

- One group of spies found that the land was really good for growing great crops, including grapes and figs.

- They found the army and the cities were strong, but with God's help they thought they could take it over.

- The other group were scared and lied about what they had seen.

- They said that the land didn't produce much food and that the people in Canaan were giants.

- They said that even with God on their side they couldn't win.

- They lied because they were scared, and their lies caused a lot of trouble for Moses and upset God.

Craft   *Good land*

You will need:

- paper

- pens and crayons

- some maps

Put some maps on tables for the group to look at and to get ideas from. Then ask the children to each draw a map of Canaan, showing all the following things:

streams and rivers	woods and forests
fields of crops	grapes and vines
towns and cities	roads and paths

Talk

God doesn't want us to lie because it causes problems for everyone. Moses had a lot of trouble with the people after the spies lied about the land of Canaan. If we tell lies instead of the truth we cause pain and make ourselves feel bad. God knows that when we lie, it is usually found out, and we end up in more trouble than at first. We should all do what God expects and speak the truth, not lies.

Memory chant

The next chant to add to the others:

Be honest when you speak.

Prayer idea

You will need:

- paper
- pens

Give each group member a small piece of paper and a pen. Ask the children to sit quietly while you play a quiet worship song on tape. Ask them to think of lies they have told that have upset other people, and to write the names of the people they lied to on their piece of paper. Then say this:

Father God, we are sorry for the lies we have told.
We are sorry for all these people we have hurt with our lies.
Father God, we know you do not want us to tell lies.
Help us to think before we speak,
and always to speak the truth.
Amen.

Songs

Lord, you put a tongue in my mouth
I'm sorry
Let us sing and praise God
Don't be an actor

9. Speak Truth.

Chant
Be honest when you speak.

Some spies said they found

ragesp

g _ _ _ _ _

tromsegpanea

p _ _ _ g _ _ _ _ _ _

sigf

f _ _ _ _

and

tiisce

c _ _ _ _ _ _

other spies said they found

dab ndal

b _ _ _ l _ _ _

and

snigat

g _ _ _ _ _ _

WHY I LIE fill this in...

_____
_____
_____ .

Finish this PRAYER...

truth   lies   tell

Dear God,
Help me to
always tell the
_____ and

never _____

_____ .

Amen.

God wants
us to tell
the truth.

Session 10   Com 10 – Be satisfied _____

Theme

'Do not desire anything others own.'

God has given us all we need, and we should learn to be satisfied.

Active game

Wants and needs

Ask the group to stand. They should remain standing if they don't want the item you mention, crouch down if they want it but don't need it, and sit on the floor if they need it. You may want to stop after each one and mention whether you think it is a want or a need:

food	a new bike
CD player	Action Man toy
home	video
new doll	family
computer	drink
parent/s	friends
money	love

Talk

There are many things we may want, but we don't really need them all. We might want to have all the latest fashionable clothing to look good, but that isn't really important. God has promised to give us all we need, and we shouldn't always want more.

Game

Quick words

Have two volunteers out at the front. Each one must say a word on the subject you give them (see below) without repeating a word or hesitating for too long. The one who comes back with another word quicker will be the winner. Repeat the game with another pair and so on as time allows.

toys and games	things at home
money	things I want
computers	TV

Discussion

Twenty years on

Lead the group as you all talk about what they would like to have and be doing in 20 years' time. Some will want to have lots of money, a big home, and expensive cars. Try to help them talk about the following:

- Who would you want to care about in 20 years' time?
- Is it really good to have lots of money?
- Can having lots of money really make you happy?
- Are people we love and who love us more important than belongings?

Story

Big, big barns!

Tell this version of the story taken from Luke 12:13-21, with the children saying 'big, big barns' every time you mention barns. This is a story that Jesus told. He wanted the people who heard it to think about what was most important to them. It is a story about barns *(big, big barns)*.

There was once a farmer who was doing very well. He had barns *(big, big barns)* which each year he filled with lots of grain. He sold the grain from his barns *(big, big barns)* and made a lot of money. As one year passed and another one began he became richer and richer thanks to all the grain in his barns *(big, big barns)*. His barns *(big, big barns)* became so full that the man started to worry about where to put all the grain. He decided that he would have even bigger barns *(big, big barns)* built so that he could make more money and live a lovely life. He wanted the new barns *(big, big barns)* so he could show off and enjoy real luxury. He got the builders in to pull down the old barns *(big, big barns)* and soon the new barns *(big, big barns)* were ready to be filled with lots of grain to make the farmer lots of money. He was very excited as he thought about all the great new things his new barns *(big, big barns)* and the money he would make would bring him. He wanted more, and more, and more. But the night the new barns *(big, big barns)* were filled with grain, something very sad happened – the man died.

Jesus explained that wanting more had taken over his life, and he had forgotten that God gives us all we need and we don't have to keep wanting more and more.

Quiz

The 10 Com race

Ask all the children to sit on the floor in three teams, with one person from each team standing in front of the groups. Then ask each team in turn a question, with the standing team member taking a step forward if the team answers correctly. The winning team will be the one whose representative is furthest forward. These questions cover all the themes in this series of 10 Com outlines, and may need a little introduction or explanation :

1. Which messenger from God prayed for fire? *(Elijah)*
2. Who were Elijah's enemies? *(followers of Baal)*
3. What pretend God did the people build when Moses was away? *(gold calf)*
4. What did Moses see burning? *(bush)*
5. Peter made a lame man walk in the name of who? *(Jesus)*
6. What did Jesus do on the Sabbath? *(healed a woman)*
7. What did Joseph's father buy him? *(coat)*
8. What upset Joseph's brothers? *(his dreams)*
9. Who was Abel's older brother? *(Cain)*
10. What did Cain do to Abel? *(killed him)*
11. What happened to the water at the wedding? *(turned to wine)*
12. What did God tell his army not to do? *(touch anything)*
13. What fruit did the spies see? *(grapes, figs, pomegranates)*
14. What did the rich man build bigger? *(barns)*
15. What are the 10 Coms? *(God's ten rules)*

Memory chant

Add this final phrase:

Have no greed in what you seek.

The full chant

Say the chant all together:

He is the only God.
Don't worship the odd.
Be careful what you say.
Have a restful day.
Honour Mum and Dad.
Don't murder or do bad.
Adults – stay together.
Don't steal things ever.
Be honest when you speak.
Have no greed in what you seek.

Prayer

Say this prayer together. You may need to copy it or write it out large enough for all the group to see:

Our Father God, thank you for all you give to us.
Thank you for your rules that help us.
Thank you for your forgiveness that cleans us.
Thank you for your love that covers us.
Thank you for all you give us.
Amen.

Songs

Ask the group members to choose their favourites from those you have sung over the weeks.

10. Be Satisfied.

Remember – God gives us all we need.

Chant

Have no greed in what you seek.

WISH LIST...

If I was rich I would have _____

Complete the picture

The Rich Man and his Big Barns

FINISH THIS PRAYER

Satisfied you need me

Thank you, God, that ___ give ___ all I ___ to be really ___.

Amen.